UNCOVERING *Toxic* JOURNEYS

Short Stories Letting You Know You're Not Alone

Samaria Janae Witherspoon

This Book Belongs To

____

Dedications

This book is dedicated to every woman that's looked in the mirror and questioned her worth and self-respect. To every woman that thought she was a monster at moments because of her own toxic ways. To every woman that has cried in the car about her situation, but wiped her tears and walked into work smiling like nothing ever happened. To every woman that's trying to heal from her own bullshit. To every woman that's been struggling trying to hold it together and keep it together. To every woman looking to learn more about herself, in the past, present and future. To every woman that's been on her knees crying to God, asking him, "Why me?" This book is to help you see that it's not only you but me, her, and her too. I dedicate this to you.

Acknowledgments

First and foremost, let me say thank You God. This journey that I've been on would not be attainable without the strength from God. I experienced depression, anxiety, sleepless nights, migraines, weight loss, etc. during my journey and I don't think I would've made it without him. I'm so humbled and grateful to God for giving me the strength to be vulnerable and share my story, experiences, interpretations, and encounters with the world.

To my mother, Sharon. I literally worship your grounds ma. Thank you for everything. You had my front, back and answer to any question or problem I posed to you. This is for you. This is for us. If I win, you win.

To my father, Johnny. My protector. The first man that ever showed me what love truly is. Thank you for being everything that I needed you to be when I needed it. I know as a man, it's hard to understand all these mixed feminine feelings, but I can honestly say you were the best supporter. Your baby girl loves you.

To my sister, Erika. Thank you for the pivotal role you play in my life. A true big sister. Always telling me what I need to hear and not what I want. Thank you for brainstorming with me and hearing my random thoughts. I always know you're going to be a straight shooter with me, and for that, I thank you and love you.

To my niece and nephew, Teighlor and Jaxson. Y'all are growing so fast and I'm so freaking happy to be your auntie. Y'all are my favorite little people in this world and that will never change. Everything that I am and will become is for you. I wrote every line with y'all in the back of my mind. Thank you for being two of my biggest motivators. I love y'all for life.

To my cousins, Quita, Yadi and Dimiao, y'all listened to my vent sessions and brainstormed with me literally at any and every time I can think. On any day at any minute, y'all were available and I'm grateful for that. I love y'all and thank you for being my favorites.

To my two best friends, Chelsey and Morgan. I love y'all to pieces. Y'all literally wiped my tears and picked me up during my battle. Please know that your selflessness and compassion was and is greatly appreciated. Y'all experienced every moment with me, and I'll never forget it. Who knew Howard University would give me two new sisters? We are locked in for life girls and I can't wait to continue to take on the rest of life with y'all.

To the remaining members of my family and friends, thank you all. The support you guys provide does not go unnoticed. I appreciate you all more than you would ever know or understand. I love you all for life.

To my clients, past, present and future... learning more about you helps me learn more about myself. Because of each of you all, I survived. I look at the world in such a better and gentler light. Thank you for trusting me on your journey. Our time shared is precious, confidential, sacred and unmatched.

To a special someone... I remember when we talked, you told me I would thank you one day for our plan. When you used to say that I cringed inside because I hated the idea of it, but now I see. We were right. The plan worked out more than we could have ever imagined, so thank you. Thank you for my newfound growth. Thank you for allowing me to see myself and love me a little bit more. I appreciate you and I will always love you.

Authors Note

The following stories are no representation of one single person, client or myself. It is a combination of several experiences and outcomes spoken from the context of one individual. Similarities of a situation spoken in first person, with a name, place or thing are completely coincidental and was written for the purpose of creating a storyline.

Contents

Permission:

\ pər-ˈmi-shən | noun

the act of permitting

I think it's important to state or think about where you are right now. Honestly, sometimes we get so caught up in trying to cope with our problems and live "our best life" that we never really sit in the fact of where we are currently. Often we're so wrapped up in the idea of where we want to be that we lose focus on where we really are. So right now, this day, this minute, this second, I give you the permission to be vulnerable and admit where you are... whether it's trying to heal from a heart break, struggling with your father's death, fighting demons on your job (that you don't even want to be at), contemplating on where you went wrong with a friend, stressing about how you're going to pay your child's day care bill, burning from the STD your boyfriend that "loves you and is sorry" gave you by cheating, mentally exhausted from the Facebook argument you just got done engaging in, tired from being on your feet because you just worked 12 long damn hours, still trying to figure out if you should go back to school or not, mad because your best friend just announced she's having a baby before you, hooked on drugs and cannot find your way of putting them down, exhausted because your baby daddy just won't act right and do his part... whatever the case may be, be honest with yourself and embrace your situation because that's the only way you will heal from your toxic ways. Trust me.. you are not alone. So now that you have the permission, where are you right now?

*I am currently battling*____________________
____
____
____
____

Learning More About Me and My Toxicity

When reading this section, I want you to focus on you, yourself and your past. I want you to learn more about your past so that you can begin to unlearn certain toxic behaviors, routines, and thoughts you have in the present. Each novel shares a story about a subject that we often overlook and misunderstand. The subjects are random but very important to grasp. They're important because I feel that these subjects make up most parts of our hurt and toxic behaviors. So open up your mind to each subject and allow yourself to be empathetic and inquisitive.

Toxic

/'täksik/ | adjective

very harmful or unpleasant in a pervasive or insidious way.

Let's do it. You ready? Let's have the conversation. Let's first start off by asking yourself what is toxic? What does it look like? What does it sound like? What does it feel like? I know... it's hard to define toxic because what you may see as toxic, I may feel is completely normal. At the beginning, middle and end of the day, we know when shit gets way too hectic. When it becomes disrespectful, uncomfortable, and unhealthy, that's when it becomes toxic.

Toxic is "ghosting" someone instead of apologizing when you're wrong. Toxic is knowing that you want nothing more than a late night call for sex with someone, but you choose to drag them along to believe you see an entire life that consists of marriage and children. Toxic is playing the victim to every situation, even the ones you created. Toxic is putting your hands on someone instead of explaining your feelings with your words. Toxic is hanging up on someone screaming "Fuck you" then calling 2 hours later, apologizing and asking them what they want to eat. Toxic is a work environment that consists of nothing but gossip and unknown reports to HR. Toxic is belittling a friend because you had a rough day. Toxic is gaslighting your partner to get a reaction. Toxic is trolling someone on social media. Toxic is sleeping with your best friend's boyfriend. Toxic is consistently breaking the promises you made even after you apologized a million times. Toxic is your mother forcing you to babysit your younger siblings while she chooses to party and bullshit. Toxic is being emotionally unavailable. Toxic is being enabled all your life. Toxic is only caring about yourself. Toxic is trying to control everyone and everything. Toxic is feeding off of gossip and drama 100% of the time. Toxic is consistently lying about something, whether it's big or small. Toxic is the inability to be happy for someone else other than yourself. Toxic is using someone's past as a weapon. Toxic is not respecting someone's boundaries or personal space. Toxic is diminishing. Toxic is uncomfortable. Toxic is draining.

I don't know how we got to the point of toxicity being normalized. It's literally a joke, especially to the millennials and generation Z. People have subjected themselves to so much negativity that it's sad. Toxic is all fun and games until you're the one going through it, trying to pick up the pieces of your life. Let me remind you that toxic isn't cute and it damn sure isn't fun. It's unnecessary and draining. Whenever it even comes close to feeling toxic, find the nearest exit. I don't care if we're talking about a job,friendship, relationship, etc.; nothing is worth your sanity. Protect it at all costs.

Some results of toxicity:
Low Self-Esteem
Depression
Damaging relationships/friendships
Anxiety
Uncontrollable rage
Inability to trust
Inability to communicate
Inability to commit

Childhood Trauma

/ˈCHīldˌho͝od ˈtrômə/ | noun

The experience of an event by a child that is emotionally painful or distressful, which often results in lasting mental and physical effects

Okay, brace yourself sis. This is sometimes one of the most complicated things we as adults struggle with facing. Although it's one of the hardest, it's also one of the most important things for us to come to terms with. Why though? Because we owe it to our adult selves to live a fulfilling life. By facing our childhood traumas, it allows us to unlearn toxic bullshit. It also prevents us from carrying extra baggage. When we ignore our childhood traumas, we only put band-aids on our bleeding wounds. We try to be gentle and clean the wound as much as possible while it still aches. But guess what? Just like any other bleeding wound that is covered with a band-aid, the band-aid wears off. Why does it wear off? Because it's full and messy. Sometimes, the blood drops out on us and other people. It causes us to get dirty in areas we never intended. What do I mean by that? It's simple... hurt people, hurt people. When the blood drops out on you, you start dealing with all types of shit. That may look like depression all because your father sexually assaulted you. When the blood drops out on other people, you are now causing other people to deal with the effects of your trauma. That may look like you constantly cheating on your partner because you never felt worthy growing up.

Listen, we all have a story sis. Maybe yours is a little messier than others, or maybe not. You don't have to sweep it under the rug. As much as you try to, you just can't. Sweeping it under the rug is something like a toddler trying to play hide-n-seek. You ever notice they hide in the most obvious places, but for some odd reason, they feel they are in the most top-secret place? They stick out like a sore thumb. That's what happens when we try to hide our childhood trauma. So what's the tea sis? Were you neglected? Were you homeless at one point? Were you molested by your uncle? Were you suicidal at one point because you were bullied as a kid? Were you emotionally abused by your father? Were you a witness to domestic violence of your mother? Did you hide an abortion at a young age? Did you go to jail? Did you find out that your uncle is really your dad and your dad is really your uncle? What was it? I'm not here to judge. I'm only here to help. My best advice for you is to find a therapist right now and commit yourself to healing from your childhood trauma.

I (insert name) _______________ commit myself to attempting to find a therapist to begin healing from my childhood trauma.

The Childhood Monster

/mon-ster/| noun

a person who excites horror by wickedness, cruelty, etc.

I hope you feel me when I say this, but FUCK YOU. Disrespectfully. You took something from me that I'll never get back. I was so innocent, and you... you took advantage of me. Now here I am 15 years later, toxic as fuck because an insensitive, dirty butt ass man was too horny for his own good. One thing about me is that I love my family so much that I would rather take your identity to the grave than have them send you to the grave (because that's exactly what they would do). And you know what's crazy, I still look at you to this day. You try to smile and laugh like nothing ever happened, but I know your guilty conscience eats you up. It has to! I hate how I start to stutter and sweat every time I'm around you. You make my skin crawl. You are disgusting. You evil ass predator. I see karma eating you up though, so I try not to even wish bad on you. Often, I sit and wonder, am I really doing a good deed by protecting my family or am I being selfish? Because what about the other little girls I see you in contact with? Hell, what about your KIDS? Every time I'm around you and I see kids; I ALWAYS try to come play with them to distract them from you. I ALWAYS do. I feel like it's only right, but is what I'm doing right? This seems selfish. Fuck man. I'm over here border line about to have an anxiety attack. You see what you did to me? I guess I feel so guilty and then I get so angry because I let a monster like you make me feel guilty. You're really not worth it though. Just know I am not that same little girl anymore. Even though I still remember the day as vivid as yesterday, I am a grown ass woman. A grown healed woman at that. You can't fuck with me now. This right here, it's not yours. It was never yours from the jump and it never will be. I'm going to end this by saying I hope you get the help you need. I will pray for you. I pray for every other child that comes in contact with you. I pray long and I pray hard. Just remember that I didn't write this letter for you. I wrote it for me and my own healing. Take care.

*If you had the chance, what would you to say to your childhood monster?*________________

____

____

____

A Father and Mother's Love

/ləv/ | noun

a protective and possessive affection which a mother and father will typically display towards their child throughout their life

The purest form of love. So many people downplay the role a mother and father play in one's life, but I'm here to tell you that it is the biggest divergent on how you will perceive love, strength, relationships, men, work, just about everything. Let's just take a moment to think about the kind of mother and father you had. Think about their personality and traits, how they would engage with others, their intimate relationship, how often they would tell you they loved you, how often y'all would spend time together, their career choices, their favorite shows and songs, their stride, every small detail. Then take a moment and think about yourself, your qualities, traits, relationships, etc. Unconsciously we grow up repeating the same patterns of our parents. Both bad and good, which is why we must be truthful when looking in the mirror assessing ourselves and our behaviors. If it's something good that we wish to repeat, then by all means, use what you know to grow. Capitalize off what's already been taught. If it's a curse that you wish to break, then be careful and be intentional. Although we could be here in this section for the remainder of the book, I only want you to think, recognize and draw up a plan to act. That's it. That's all. Do it for you. Do it for your kids. Do it for your grandkids.

"There's no way I can pay you back, but the plan is to show you that I understand. You are appreciated." – Tupac Shakur

Generational Curse

/ˌjenəˈrāSH(ə)nəl ˈkərs/ | noun

the cumulative effect on a person of things that their ancestors did, believed, or practiced in the past, and a consequence of an ancestor's actions, beliefs, and sins being passed down

The first and most important note I want to make is that although our ancestors passed down generational trauma that we are trying to heal from, they also passed down generational strengths. Acknowledge that. Our ancestors made the blueprint that we attempt to live by. Keep in mind that they didn't have a manual on how to survive; they just knew that's what they had to do. I give all the honor and respect to my ancestors. They underwent things that I could not imagine facing nor come close to even overcoming. So, take this time now to give thanks to your ancestors. Remember, we are our ancestor's wildest dreams.

Now let me give you an example of a generational curse. Your great-grandmother may have been a victim of racism and abuse. Because of the abuse and trauma she experienced, she may have developed symptoms of depression, anxiety or even a substance abuse problem. Your great-grandmother then birthed your grandmother and your great aunts and uncles. Due to the toxic household that they grew up in seeing your great-grandmother struggling with her depression, anxiety and alcoholism, they too struggled with the same issues. They are resentful of love, safety and compassion. This may look like them sleeping with multiple partners filling the voids that their mother never touched on, neglecting their parental duties because they simply don't know how to parent because they were never shown the proper way or moving far away from their families because they hate the thought of all the toxic shit they experienced. Then you know what happens? Your grandmother somehow births your mother. Your mother grows up seeing the same shit that your grandmother experienced. Your mother has more resources than your grandmother had, but she too struggles with her parenting skills, alcoholism, sense of relationships and safety. Then guess who comes along? You. You grow up wondering why you have this mean streak of anger, inability to control your weakness of toxic men, resentment towards your own mom, estranged sisters, brothers and cousins that you don't meet until you're an adult and a strong desire to smoke weed and drink alcohol every chance you get. Life seems so hard because you can't keep a stable job because your boss is always saying you have a bad attitude. You're always attracted to men that seems to cheat on you and on top of that, you just had a baby, and now you're struggling mentally, financially, and emotionally. That my dear is a prime example of how generational curses work. Do you see the extent that it has not only on your life but your children's life, your grandchildren's life and so forth? The saying, "hurt people hurt people" is what generational curses do, which is why it's most important for us to heal. We have to heal and do the work so that we can stop the same recycled patterns. Those patterns are so old, and tired. They're draining. We've dealt with them long enough. Let's break the chain. We have enough resources and support to do it. When we heal ourselves, we heal our children, our grandchildren and so forth. We are capable. We are strong. We are worthy. We are important. We are the future.

*I am breaking the generational curse of*____

____

____

______________________________________.

The Mirror

/ˈmirər/ | noun

a reflective surface, now typically of glass coated with a metal amalgam that reflects a clear image

Do me a favor, go to the bathroom right now. No like seriously, get up and walk to the bathroom right now. Look in the mirror and tell me what you see. I don't want to hear the basic things about your hair or your acne or anything like that. Tell me what you really see. Tell me if you see someone that is happy and then rate it on a scale of 1-10. 1 being miserable, 10 being ecstatic. Tell me if you see someone that loves their family and tells them that on a regular basis. Tell me if you see a good friend and if you do, say out loud 1 thing that you have done for a friend in the last week. If you don't, tell me one thing you want to work on when being a better friend. Tell me if you see someone that is satisfied with their job and then give me 1 high about your job and 1 low. Tell me if you see a great mother and if you do, tell me 2 reasons why you are a good mother and if you don't tell me 2 reasons why you aren't a good mother. Tell me if you see a person that is grieving. If you do, say out loud "I, ___ (your name) genuinely miss ____(your deceased love) and I am in the process of accepting that they are no longer physically with me, but they will forever live in my mind and heart." If you're not, think of 3 people that you're grateful for that is still here with you today. Tell me if you see someone that is broken. If you do, tell me what broke you and if you don't, say a word for those that are broken. Tell me if you see someone that is currently on the financial battlefield. If you do, write down 1 way you plan to overcome your financial problem; if you don't, tell me one way that you're financially free. Tell me if you see a beautiful soul. And by a beautiful soul, I mean you treat others how they want to be treated and you love and care genuinely for those that are connected to you. Tell me if you see someone that is single, married, playing side chick, in multiple relationships or in a relationship with themself. Tell me if you see a person dealing with substance abuse. If you are, say this, "Hi! My name is _____ and I'm addicted to ______." If you aren't, pray for those who are. Tell me if you see someone battling depression or anxiety. If you do, ask yourself how long you plan to battle it and if you're willing to do something about it. If you don't take a minute and say "Thank you God" because that is such a blessing and I'm proud of you. Okay, come on. Tell me. What do you see?

"Lately I been feeling like it's me vs. me."
- Moneybagg Yo

Stink

/stiNGk/ | verb

a strong unpleasant smell; a stench

If no one else has told you today, I'm here to tell you that your shit stinks too. Stop trying to look across the street at your neighbor's front porch and take a chance to sweep around your own. Yeah, you may have it somewhat together, but it's not all together. Stop pointing the finger at them when there is 4 more fingers pointing back at you. Have you ever thought about you being the problem? Yes, maybe they are a little toxic, but what are you? What makes you so different? Something initially connected them to you, so are you really different? I'm not here to make you second guess yourself... I'm only here to make you check yourself. It's okay to be in tune with yourself, but the goal is to be so in tune with yourself that you are also able to hold yourself accountable. Now that's growth. That's when you're the shit. When you know you may be the shit, but you have a little shit with you and you're capable of cleaning up your own shit? Whew! That's when you become untouchable.

We have to stop ignoring our own red flags and pointing out others. We are not perfect. We are going to screw up. It's life. We all have areas to perfect. It's completely normal. It's nothing to hide. We may fall short, but the most important thing is that we get up. Ignoring our own red flags and normalizing our bullshit only hurts ourselves. It hurts us and prohibits us from touching and reaching levels that we can reach. It's okay not to be okay sometimes. Just be willing and ready to do the work.

"I know you'd like to think your shit don't stank, but lean a little bit closer, see roses really smell like poo-poo-ooh. Yeah, roses really smell like poo-boo-ooh"
-Outkast

I Apologize

/əˈpäləˌjīz/ | verb

to express regret for something that one has done wrong

Sometimes I sit in bed crying and asking God, why. Like why did I do the evil shit I did in the past? As a woman, I can admit I've done a lot of horrible shit. The thing is, I'm no longer embarrassed because I'm here to own it and I know for a fact that I am not who I once was. I will give myself credit and say I didn't do it because I'm a horrible person it was that.. I was still growing. I couldn't see past my own bullshit. Yes, I know the past is the past and there is nothing we can do to rewind time. I'm not trying to rewind anything, but in order for me to move forward, I have to say I'm sorry. And this time, I mean it. I'm sorry to every friend that I didn't come through for like I should have. I can admit in the past, I felt a sense of entitlement and it wasn't right. It wasn't fair to my friends that actually were good friends. I'm not sure if the bonds will ever rekindle, but I wish you well. I'm sorry to every family member that I made second guess my loyalty and love. Please know it was never my intention and I do genuinely adore you. I'm here now and I promise I will do everything to prove it. I'm sorry to every lover I may have mislead, cheated on or manipulated. It wasn't my true character. I'm really a straight shooter that adores compassion, communication, consistency and commitment. I was smelling and eating up my own shit at the time, and now that I had a dose of it… it doesn't feel or taste that good. I hope you can forgive me and find the woman that is truly for you. I apologize to every person that I may have come in contact with and rubbed the wrong way. Whatever the situation was, I take accountability for my part and I apologize. I don't want to live with beef nor hatred and it ends today.

I'm not the same person I was. Although I'm still crazy, bubbly, loud, outgoing and outspoken… my values changed. My taste changed. I hope you all can forgive me for who I once was and allow this new version to shower you with kindness and compassion. I won't let you down and once again, I apologize.

It's so hard for us to say those two words, but we have to. How can we move forward without taking accountability for our past? Don't just do it for you, do it for your children and future grandchildren. No one deserves to heal from your generational bullshit and hate. Say you're sorry and mean it.

I apologize for ______________________________

____

____

(Be transparent and apologize for some of the wrongdoings you may have done in the past).

Understanding The Basics

So now that we have touched on concepts that help us learn more about our inner selves and pasts, I want you to focus on these subjects. These subjects influence our beliefs, mindsets, relationships, and career choices. Like before, they're at complete random, but very important. These concepts force us into our "dark places." So read this in hopes of escaping your dark place by seeing the light.

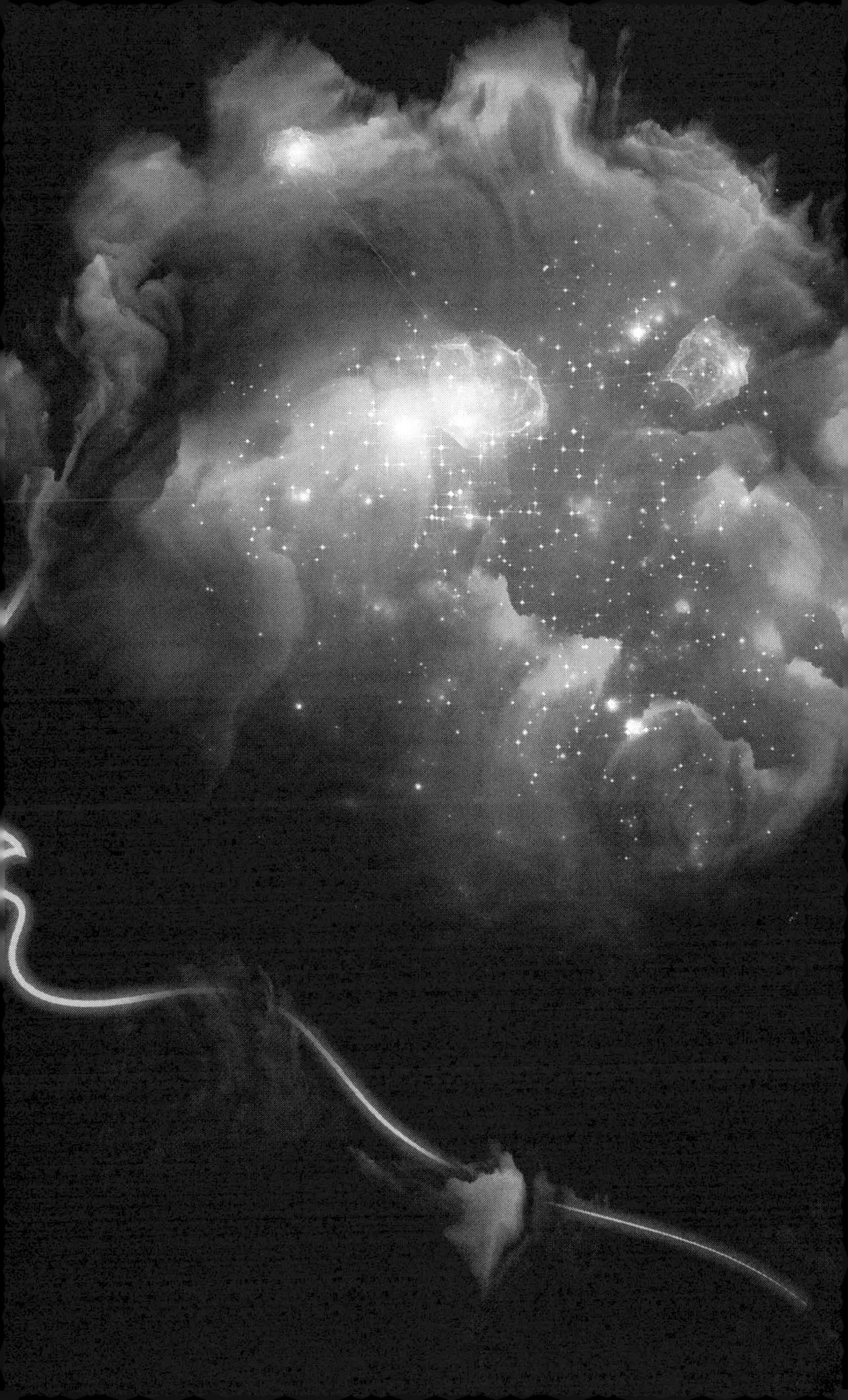

Family

/ fam-uh-lee/ | noun

any group of people closely related by blood or marriage, as parents, children, uncles, aunts, and cousins

GANG, GANGGGGGG BABYYYYYYY! OMG. I'm so ratchet. But in all actuality, my family is my gang. I love them until death do us part. It actually might be unhealthy to love them as much as I do. From my immediate family to my cousins, uncles, great aunts, all that. Often online, I see people question what family is? I feel like a family is a group of individuals that love, support, motivate, and enjoy you. Within your family, it is composed of different spirits, some healthy and some not. For the healthy ones, gravitate closer to them. Love them. Support them. Build a legacy with them. Being family and connected is something that no one can take away nor change. You and your family share memories and experiences that probably no one will understand, know about or maybe even respect BUT y'all. Don't take that for granted. Cherish it and hold it tight.

For the unhealthy spirits, run! I'm not an advocate for someone to stay connected to people simply because of a title. If you feel that they don't serve your energy... leave them exactly where they are. Family or not. It's not our responsibility to carry toxic energy and spirits, so by all means, SEPARATE YOUR SELF. They may say things like, "You think you're better than us" or "Oh, she acts too good to fool with us." You know what? Fuck them. You don't owe them anything. You probably gave them genuine love at one point, and they abandoned it, so who cares about their opinion? Nothing is wrong with loving people from a distance. People serve different purposes in your life and that goes for family too. Moral of the story: family can be toxic AF too and you should not feel bad for eliminating them out our circle.

"Nobody wins when the family feuds."- Jay Z.

Friends

/friend/ | noun

a person whom one knows and with whom one has a bond of mutual affection, typically exclusive of sexual or family relations

"Friends! How many of us have them? Friends! The ones you can depend on. Friends!" I know we all know the song, but that was a real question. How many do you have? And I'm not talking about a person that you can go to the bar, grab a drink and gossip with all night. Or the "friend" that is excited to hear about you and your boyfriend breaking up and now they're helping you send a text message to him. Nor am I talking about the "friend" that takes cute pictures with you and posts them on Instagram and then you don't hear from her again until she needs something. I'm talking about a real genuine friend. You know, the friend that doesn't mind coming over to your house to do absolutely nothing or may even help you organize your closet. The friend that was there when your grandmother passed away. She told you what she was going to do to support you instead of saying, "Let me know if you need something." The friend that you can go to brunch, lunch or dinner with, and she doesn't care to gossip because she's talking to you about where she sees you in the next month or so. The friend that never changed on you throughout your whole pregnancy and still wants to babysit little Juju. The friend that calls you late at night and says, "Girl, Mathew just pissed me off, can you please pray with me?" The friend that has never come to your house empty-handed if she was in the position to bring something. The friend that's there to celebrate your new car, raise, divorce settlement, photoshoot, closing and even your hair's new growth. The friend that you had a disagreement with on Friday and 2 weeks later, you are yet to see a subliminal post on Instagram yet. The friend that is sitting outside the waiting room to support you after you told her that you felt your vagina itching a little bit. The friend that does not support you sleeping with married men because she cares more about your character and values than some temporary dick. The friend that caught your man looking at her in a flirtatious way and addresses him first and then comes back to tell you how she just cursed him the fuck out. The friend that will pull you to the side and let you know that you don't smell as fresh as your usual instead of running to the other person in the friend group to talk shit about you. The friend that was able to tell you your wig was a little crooked instead of writing in her

GroupMe about it leaning sideways. The friend that you expressed your hurt about your boyfriend to, and she demanded that y'all take a trip to just relax your mind. I'm talking about those type of friends. How many do you have? 10? 5? 4? 2? 1? Or maybe even none huh? Regardless of the number, don't feel bad. Real is rare and sometimes less is more. Remember that.

And one HUGE point that I want to highlight is... in order to have a friend, you have to be a friend. Let me say it again, IN ORDER TO HAVE A FRIEND... YOU HAVE TO BE A FRIEND. For example, you can't expect your friend to always celebrate your high moments when you are nowhere to be found for hers. You can't expect your friend to share her personal business with you when the last time she told you something, you went and said something to Briana about it. You can't expect something when you give absolutely nothing. But let me say that I know we all have our days and sometimes you just can't give anything and that's okay. With life happening the way it is, you can't always give energy to certain situations. In cases like that, that is okay. And when you do have a situation like that, your "friend" is supposed to understand, but just remember that can't be your excuse all the time.

Another special note I want to make is if you constantly see yourself in the same ring with a "friend" fighting the same problems, then simply get out of the ring. Don't try to fight them, don't go and tell all the secrets you all shared, don't try to mess with their boyfriend, don't go make a subliminal post on Instagram, just simply get out the ring with them. It's not hard. Friends are supposed to be there to help you through problems, not constantly making a problem with you. We use the term "friend" way too loosely nowadays and get mad when they don't live up to our expectations. It's okay to have associates, co-workers, classmates, or a going out partner; those are still things. To label someone as a friend, you're giving them a huge role within your life and I believe people take that for granted. So now let me ask you, how many friends do you have and what kind of friend are you?

My friends would describe as ____________ ____________________________________.

I have ____________________ friends and I would describe them as ________________ ____________________________________.

Enablers

/eˈnāblər/ | noun

a person who encourages negative or self-destructive behavior in another

I gave you the book definition, but in all actuality... enablers are people that make you feel so good, but are no good for you. They're really toxic AF. They are the ones that will cheer you on when you're running to the wrong side of the court. They're the people that will pat you on the back right after you failed your test and say, "Your teacher should have prepared you a little more." They're the people that will lead you to self-destruction. Growing up, my mom always told me, "Right or wrong, I'll have your back in front of the world, but behind closed doors... I'm going to tell you that you were wrong." That right there let me know that she would never accept something just because I was her daughter. Yes, she would support me and have my back, but she was also willing to correct me. Way too often, we have these "family members" and "friends" that enable us. They make us feel like we do no wrong and that everyone else is the problem. Although it's hard, we have to stay away from those type of people. They will never allow us to grow into our full potential. Ever had a big sister or cousin that's always ready to jump up to do every and anything for you? I mean, every time you call, no matter if it's the dumbest idea, they're ready to ride. That's a red flag! Yes, you need people that's down to ride, but you really need people to look at you and say, "Now Drina, that's stupid and I cannot allow you to do this." That's the energy we really need. Or you need people to say, "I can teach you how to do it, but I cannot do it for you." I mean how else are you supposed to know how to survive in this evil world if you don't learn? Mommy, big sister or cousin won't always be there. Most of all, how will we be able to pass down the torch to our children or our grandchildren? We won't be able to if we've been enabled all our life.

Make sure you have people in your circle to challenge you from a place of love. They should encourage growth and positivity. They shouldn't be afraid to tell you no or to question your doings. You both should feel solidified enough in your relationship to know the criticism is for the best and not the worst. Embrace the fact that some people see things that we simply cannot at times.

It's a difference between being spoiled and being enabled. We just have to find the fine line in between. And yes, it's hard. Like I said before, being enabled feels so good but it is really no good for us. Not in the long run, at least. Yes, get a lending hand, but learn how to regulate your own lives and situations. We control our own destinies.

"We cripple people who are capable of walking because we choose to carry them."
- Christie Wallace

Intentions

/ in-ten-shuhns/ | noun

the purpose or attitude toward the effect of one's actions or conduct

In this section, I want to focus on how to manage negative encounters without it ending in turmoil. Facts are facts. You are not going to agree with everyone. You are not going to like everything someone says or does and someone is going to make you feel a certain type of way. It's life and it will happen. And to be completely transparent, I didn't really think this through until I was faced with issues of my own with a previous friend. If you're like me, then when your feelings are hurt, they're hurt. When you're passionate about something, you're passionate and you don't mind verbalizing your thoughts. I know everyone isn't as vocal about their feelings, but I must admit I was and still am. As an adult that plans to maintain that friendship, job, relationship, or marriage, you have to focus on the intentions of the person rather than the disagreement at hand. So let me give you an example. Let's say you are in a friend group along with 2 other girls. Lately, you have been going through the regular motions of life and you've been a little on edge. Friend #2 decides to go to friend #3 to talk about your recent behavior that she has witnessed. She expresses that you have been condescending when talking with them, not keeping up with the cleanliness of your house and have not been responsive when they call/text. A week later friend #3 approaches you and tells you how friend #2 came to her and expressed some concerns. Friend #3 then makes the statement that you have been acting "different" lately and asked if you were okay. You instantly become defensive because you feel that your friends have been talking behind your back. Secondly, you don't feel that you have been acting differently. You end the conversation with friend #3 and you are furious. You then question yourself on why friend #2 didn't just approach you with her "concerns." I mean y'all are all adults, right? So what was the big ordeal with her sharing how she felt about you, to you? You then question what else has been discussed behind your back. And lastly, you question why your friends assume that you have been acting differently simply because you've been going through the regular motions of life. I mean, everyone has their own problems. So what if you been a little on edge? As friends, they are supposed to recognize that you may be going through some things and be a little compassionate, right? The right thing to do would have been to ask you if everything is okay rather than discuss you among themselves.

In this exact moment, everybody has you "fucked up". So let's evaluate this. The madness first started when friend #2 voiced how she felt about you to friend #3 right? So bam, in this particular situation, your best bet is to first evaluate friend #2. You ask yourself, what are her character traits? Is this something that happens often? Is she really a messy person? Is she always in the center of drama and he say, she say? Do you think she shared her thoughts simply because she wanted to be messy and talk about you or did she really discuss it because she was genuinely concerned? Yes. The delivery was definitely wrong, but maybe the concern was genuine. We have to keep in mind that no one has a manual of how to do this thing called life. It's all about a person's intentions rather than their actual actions. Now, if she has a track of being messy and doing things like this, then yes, cut her off. But if not, why waste energy and fall out with someone that may genuinely care about you? It's not many people in this world that have PURE intentions for you, so when you find people that do...keep them around. A simple conversation will solve the problem. It needs to be a conversation discussing the intentions of each party and how to act on those intentions moving forward. Life is too short. Don't lose the real ones over petty shit.

A special note to add is that some people do not have pure intentions for you. There are really just pure evil people in the world. They have the intentions of manipulating, back-stabbing and downplaying everything about you. They may have the face of a brother, cousin, auntie, friend, co-worker, etc., but the heart of Lucifer. Be careful in choosing your circle. Be intentional.

"What's for me... is for me and what's for me... won't play about me!" - SamJ

Depression

/dəˈpreSH(ə)n/ | noun

a common and serious medical illness that negatively affects how you feel, the way you think and how you act

Depression is the inability to get out of bed for hours, day, even weeks at a time. Depression is the inability to smile and not knowing why. Depression is not wanting to talk to anyone but also not wanting to be alone. Depression is waking up in the morning only looking forward to going to bed at night. Depression is having meltdowns over the smallest issues. Depression is continuous mood swings throughout the day. Depression is being unmotivated. Depression is believing you are a burden to everyone around you, including yourself. Depression is talking to the person in your head more than the person in the room with you. Depression is crying nonstop at a time and not knowing how to control your emotions. Depression is laying on the floor, praying to God that your situation changes because you ran out of options. Depression is attempting to end your life because you don't see any other way out. Depression is drinking or smoking uncontrollably to escape your everyday emotions. Depression is the same girl that posted a picture on Facebook with the caption, "Top 2 and not # 2" with the hopes of everyone dropping heart eyes because she's been so insecure about her weight. Depression is feeling the need to constantly be on the go because you don't want to stay at home and think about your problems. Depression is going to work and not being able to fulfill your duties because you are so confused about your situation. Depression is that same flashy guy you see throwing money in the club seeking to fill a void right after his grandmother died. Depression is not having an appetite because you have too much on your mind. Depression is feeling the urge to cut yourself because you want to numb the pain you're feeling. Depression is your kid acting out at school because he feels unloved at home. Depression is "going off" on your co-worker because you are sleep-deprived. Depression overdosing on pain-killers because you don't want to feel any more pain. Depression is uncontrollable weight and hair loss due to ongoing stress. Depression is cancelling plans on your family and friends without any real explanation. Depression is the same girl posting provocative pictures on Instagram seeking reassurance and approval from the world that she is loved. Depression is sometimes loud and sometimes it's quiet. Depression is real.

If you are experiencing any of the above symptoms or anything similar, I strongly advise you to get the help you need. Depression is nothing to be ashamed of. It's something that I, she and he also experienced. It's complicated and it's not something to ignore. Ignoring it only makes your symptoms 10x worst. It's okay not to be okay. Trust me. As a mental health professional, I still have my own therapist. Why? Because I too, find myself slipping into dark places. I am no different than you. This book right here helped pull me out of a dark place by simply allowing me to vent and share my bottled-up thoughts. Get the necessary help you need and release. It's no fun carrying all of that dead weight around.

Now let me warn you and let you know that working through your depression is not easy. It's hard work. You know why? It's because you're touching all the bruised places in your past and present to avoid the same hurt in the present. Don't be afraid though. Stay consistent. Stay committed. The reward, in the long run, is worth more than anything you could ever imagine.

"Life is not about waiting for the storm to pass; it's about learning to dance in the rain."
- Vivian Green

Anxiety

/aNG'zīədē/ | noun

a feeling of worry, nervousness, or unease, typically about an imminent event or something with an uncertain outcome

Currently writing this as I'm up wide awake at 4 in the morning. I woke up and I couldn't breathe. My chest was aching; and my mind was racing too. When's the last time you felt like that? Ever had a big event or test approaching and you felt your body physically reacting? You may have started cramping, vomiting or your head instantly pounding. Or maybe you were just laid off from your job and now you're sitting in your room trying to figure out how you're going to make it financially over the course of the next month. You start feeling lightheaded, your heart is racing, you start shaking and getting the jitters, and your body starts running hot. Or maybe it was something as simple as a picture that you posted on Instagram. You thought it was cute as hell, but here it is 10 minutes later with only 3 likes. You then start to look back at the picture, finding all types of flaws that you have never seen before. These are just simple signs of dealing with anxiety. It's no joke and for some, it's uncontrollable without some type of substance or pain relief medication. Often in the black community, we sweep mental health disorders such as anxiety and depression under the rug and we're told to pray about it. Why though? I love the Lord and I'm most definitely going to pray, but why not put some work in too? We have to take care of ourselves. Experiencing anxiety is completely normal. You're not crazy nor weird. It's something that we all deal with it.

Tips For Dealing With Anxiety

1. **Focus on what is currently happening and what you can control.** In most situations, anxiety starts by overthinking. We start thinking of all different scenarios in which something could result in which puts us in a frenzy. Take a pause from all the what ifs and why's and focus on the what's and how you can deal with the situation at hand.

2. **Find support.** Sometimes all we need is a comforting voice to say, "Everything is going to be okay." We are not able to tell ourselves that because we're too busy thinking about the what if's and why's. Lean on your support system to pull you out of that dark place. Don't be ashamed.

3. **Tap into your self-care plan.** We will later discuss the importance of a self-care plan.

When you develop it, utilize it. I don't care if it's 10 p.m. or 3 in the morning. If your self-care plan says to play your favorite playlist... play it! If it says to do a quick exercise... do it for 15 minutes. It doesn't have to be extensive. You have the tools, don't be afraid to use them.

4. **Document it.** Instead of holding all your feelings and thoughts in, allow yourself to release it. I'm old-fashioned, so I'm a big advocate for a good ole pen and piece of paper. I write whatever, whenever. Some people prefer to type things in their notepads on their phones, while others like to get real fancy and record videos. Whatever way you choose, document it. It's always good to document it so when you finally pull yourself out of the dark moment; you can see the growth within. You'll know for future references how to deal with the same issue.

"Last night, I cried. Tossed and turned. Woke up with dry eyes. My mind was racing. Feet were pacing. Lord, help me please tell me what I have gotten into"- Vivian Green

Grief

/grēf/ | noun

deep sorrow from the loss of something or someone

Such a complicated process. Whew! Let me start off by saying that you have my deepest condolences if grief is something that you are currently facing. You're also in my thoughts and prayers if you are in the process of trying to help someone else heal from grief. To be very honest, grief is very rough. It's a never-ending process, especially when dealing with the death of someone. It's also something that only the person dealing with grief firsthand has the power to overcome. It's nothing anyone can say or do to permanently help someone that is dealing with grief overcome it. Let me be clear that grief is not only centered around the death of someone, but you can grieve from any loss, whether it is a break-up, job, marriage separation, business investment, monetary investment, etc. Grief is when you are facing any loss that results in a loss of love, safety, and control.

The 5 stages of grief are denial, anger, depression, bargaining, and acceptance. When grieving, you would hope to move clockwise throughout the stages, but very rarely does that happen. You may go back and forth through each stage until you are at peace with the loss. The denial stage is when you're not able to accept that what or who you once had, is no longer here. It doesn't seem real. If you lost someone to death, you might tell yourself that they went on vacation and they're coming back. You're just not able to accept the fact of what happened. You make every excuse in the world for it happening and you may blame others. You just can't see past the truth that it or they are really gone, and you will do or say anything instead of facing it. The anger stage is when you have now realized that it has happened, but you can't understand why it happened. You just can't fathom that this is something that you are experiencing, and you become extremely angry about it. This is the stage where you may resent people, things and maybe even God. You may do things that you normally wouldn't do because you're acting out of anger. This is actually a dangerous stage, and you have to be very careful when you're in this stage. Next is depression. This is when you have realized what happened and you're tired of being angry. You don't have any more energy to give. You are deeply hurt at this stage. You have so many unanswered questions and nothing can really make you feel better. It's not a single person or thing that can make you feel better. You feel empty because that thing or person is now gone. This is one of the hardest stages to pull yourself out of honestly. It takes time and a great deal of strength. Bargaining is when you have saw things for what they are, displayed your anger, felt your hurt and now you're willing to do anything to get back that thing or person. This may look like you praying to God begging him to send your child back and take your life instead. Or even telling God that you will no longer cheat on your spouse if he can send them back to you. You are willing to make any deal no matter how crazy and impossible it is. You're so vulnerable that you are willing to sacrifice anything to fill the missing void. Lastly, is acceptance. This is when you have gone through all other stages and are finally at peace. You have worked through each issue and now you are able to live somewhat "normal". It doesn't mean you forgot about the person or thing, it just means you have accepted that they are no longer here. It also doesn't mean that you won't still cry or feel any pain. It simply means you are okay with saying that the person or thing no longer exists.

Once again, you truly have my condolences if grief is something you are battling. No, things will never be the same. I can assure you that you can and will adapt to how things are destined to be though. It will take time, but you will get through it. Much love to you.

Be patient with yourself.

Karma

/ kahr-muh /| noun

seen as bringing upon oneself inevitable results, good or bad, either in this life or in a reincarnation

The baddest bitch. That's just how I'm going to start it off. Do y'all believe in karma? I remember I used to think it was something that people would say as a scare tactic, but as the years went by...I realized that karma is real. What you put in this world; you will get out. Meaning if you are constantly mean, angry, condescending, and messy. Guess what you will get back? Messy, uncomfortable, painful and overall sticky situations. One thing about karma is that it doesn't discriminate. Meaning maybe it won't affect you, but you may see it affects your mother, child, cousin, grandfather, etc. You're sitting there wondering why you can't seem to find a job that will hire you, not remembering how you just stole from your best friend. You're wondering why your child called you while she was breaking down crying. She's heartbroken because her boyfriend just cheated on her. You're angry, but you're forgetting how you slept with somebody's husband last year. You're wondering why your house was broken into out of all the houses on the road, not remembering that you just did a hit and run 3 months ago. These are just simple things, but most times... God hits you harder than what you thought you got away with. You just can't do people any type of way and then think it's okay. You just can't. And another thing about karma... it doesn't have a time limit. So yes, you may be living your best life at the moment, but by all means... karma will find its way back to you. Regardless if it's a month, year, 5 years or 10 years later. That's just how it works.

Another special note that I want to make is, stop blocking your blessings and let karma and God do its due diligence. I get it. When someone/something betrays you, you want them to feel EXACTLY how you felt (if not worst). So what do you do? You plan for revenge. Little do you know what karma and God has planned for them. Your hands do not have to get dirty in the mix. Keep it cute and clean. Because you know what happens when you get your own hands dirty? You create your own path of karma to come back. It's not worth it sis. I feel your pain, but it's just not worth it. Let karma work its magic. It never misses!

When you entertain a clown,
you become a part of the circus.

Social Media

/sōSHəl 'mēdēə/ | noun

websites and applications that enable users to create and share content or to participate in social networking

"If you are on Myspace, put me in your top 8". OMG. Do y'all remember Myspace? Social media has come so far, and I'm sure it has plans to go even further. It's scary, but it's most definitely real. Here it is 2021 and just about everyone has some sort of social media account, whether it's Facebook, Instagram, Pinterest, TikTok, Twitter, LinkedIn, Snapchat, etc. If you don't leave with understanding any part of this section, I want you to understand that your social media should promote healthiness and happiness.

Some of us only use social media for entertainment purposes while others use it for business and educational purposes. Then there are those that use social media to keep in contact with their family and friends. And some of us use it out of pure boredom. Whatever the reason may be, know that you have the right to protect your energy.

6 Tips of Promoting Healthiness and Happiness on Social Media

1. **Follow those who inspire and teach you**. Some of the most knowledgeable tips that I learned were directly from social media. You have people that don't mind giving you the keys to success and those are the ones that you should gravitate to. The travel blogger, the motivational speaker, the fashion guru, the civil rights activist, the Bitcoin CEO, the basketball wife, the Vice President... follow them. Don't be afraid to be a "fan." Your intentions on following them is not to compare your life to someone else, it's to inspire yourself to want and do more.

2. **Avoid negativity.** The stupid Facebook arguments, the controversial debates, the trolling accounts, the Karen's, the Wendy Williams's, AVOID THEM. You don't need that type of energy in your life. I'm sure you have enough bullshit in your everyday life and don't need any more from social media. If it doesn't make money or make sense, scroll right on pass it. Trust me; you're not missing out on anything.

3. **Unfriend, block and unfollow whomever whenever.** This is my biggest thing. Be unapologetic about who you choose to engage

with on social media. Don't allow someone that no longer feeds your energy to have a seat in your life. If they don't serve a purpose in your real life, then why allow them in your social media life? I'm not afraid to block or unfollow anyone. I just have no interest in certain things or people anymore. The ex-best friend, the hating in-law, the crazy ex-boyfriend, the nosey co-worker, let them go. They will probably still find a way to have a seat within your life, but make sure it's not through you.

4. **Stop wasting so much time on social media.** We all tend to sit and scroll and scroll and scroll. Before we know it, we've been on there for 2 hours straight. Do you know how much more information you could be feeding your brain with? Set timers and limits. When the timer goes off, go read a book or go clean. Do something productive. Don't get caught up in the fake hype.

5. **Only post what you want others to see.** I'm not sure if people don't know or don't care, but once you post it on social media... it's there forever. I don't care if you did press delete; it's never deleted from the clouds. Share your thoughts, cute pictures or whatever, but never post something that doesn't align with your values. I hate when people say, "It's just social media." Yes. It is only social media, but it's also what you are promoting to the world.

Your employers, children, aunties, clients, etc. are your audiences, so advertise yourself accordingly.

6. **Remember, people only post what they want you to see.** Just as well as you are only posting the best versions of yourself and life, remember that everyone else is too. Stop falling into a deep depression thinking that you're not where you're supposed to be. You have no clue what that person has gone through or really is going through. Follow to be inspired, but never to compare.

"All of y'all having more followers, than dollars and that's why I cannot relate."- Drake

The 3 C's

/THrē 'si/ |

I preach the 3 C's. I live by the 3 C's and I'll probably die by the 3 C's. I feel that they are instrumental in any healthy relationship or endeavor. Without the 3 C's I feel that you lack the basic supply of security, love, success and longevity. So what exactly are the 3 C's?

Communication

A common problem that we as humans face is that we don't know how to effectively communicate with one another. Most listen to reply and not to understand. The obvious is that we are all different individuals with our own agendas. Keeping that in the mind, we have to learn to respect everyone's individuality and opinion no matter the situation. Whether it's you at work trying to communicate with your coworker or you trying to communicate with your best friend. Learn to be patient. Learn to ask and not assume. Learn to actually listen to the other person. Learn to process the information that was given. Learn to separate feelings and facts. Learn to choose your words wisely. Learn to choose the right tone. Learn to take ownership of your own actions. Most importantly, learn how to simply be nice. Most times, it's not what you say it's how you say it.

Consistency

In this world, you cannot be afraid. You have to learn to take risks in order to prosper. How do you expect to produce the results you want without consistently putting in the work? No results? Keep working. Okay results? Keep working. Good results? Keep working. Great results? Keep working. The grind doesn't stop. This is key no matter the situation. Going on dates and spending quality time with your partner once a year won't help you two reach marriage and kids. Being a top performer at work once every blue moon won't help you get the promotion you really want. Choosing to answer the phone for your best friend 50% of the time won't help her trust you in long run. Promoting your work on social media 5 times out of the year won't help you build the brand you've been working so hard on. Washing and nourishing your hair every other month won't help you reach the hair goals that you idolize on social media. Saving $10 out of every check won't help you reach the 100,000 that you put on your vision board. Drinking water and eating healthy once every week won't help you lose the 15 pounds that you prayed to God to lose. Going over your child's homework only on the nights where you're not tired won't help your child succeed how they need. Moral of the story, you can't stop. You must keep going. And not just some of the time, but all of the time.

Commitment

If you're not giving your all; then you're wasting your time. Being committed means to be fully dedicated. Being committed means giving all your time. Being committed means giving all your energy. Being committed means blocking out distractions. Being committed means making a promise to yourself. Being committed means choosing a clear-cut path. Being committed means choosing you and the goal over and over again. Don't lose that business endeavor because you're not committing yourself. Don't lose that good man because you're not committing yourself. Don't lose that good job because you're not committing yourself. Stop wasting time and do it for your future self.

A Union Between Two

/ˈyo͞onyən/ | noun

the formation of a single political unit from two or more separate and independent units.

Let me first acknowledge that this is a safe place, but we're going to be real. Family, friends, co-workers and in-laws serve one purpose within your relationship and that's to support. That's it. That's all. Often times, I believe people forget this part within the relationship. When you are in a relationship with someone, what goes on between you two is nothing but you two's business. Yes, get advice but be careful how much you share. You may be able to forgive and move on, but other's may not. Then there's always that family, friend, co-worker, in-law that is jealous of your union and they will never feed you what you really need to hear. They will feed you what they feel you should hear. No one can understand your relationship like you can, so why bend over backwards trying to convince others what you see or feel? It's not worth it. Nothing between you and your partner has to be a secret, but everyone should not be a part of your relationship. It only causes confusion and mixed feelings. If you picked your partner, invest and build with them. Stop looking for those family members, friends, co-workers or in-laws to support. Eventually, they will come around and if they don't, they were never supposed to. Respectfully.

"All I need in the world of sin, is me and my boyfriend. Me and my boyfriend. Down to ride to the very end. Just me and my boyfriend."
- Beyonce'

Black

\ 'blak \ | adjective

being a color that lacks hue and brightness and absorbs light without reflecting any of the rays composing it

My black is beautiful. My black is strong. My black is powerful. My black is unique. My black is real. My black is resilient. My black is unapologetic. My black is fearful. My black is intimidating. My black is favorable. My black is creative. My black is a culture.

Sis, I don't care what they try to tell you about our black, but it is bold and it is necessary. We are the creators, the trendsetters, the first of the first, the best and they hate it. They hate that we always come out on top. They hate how resourceful we are and how we can and will make a way out of anything. They want us to be afraid. But we could never. We were made for this. We really are a threat to them. Don't believe me? Just take a look at Sandra Bland, George Floyd, Tamir Rice, Trayvon Martin.

This is just a reminder for you to love your black. Don't hide your black. Embrace your black. Build your black. And a special note, stop tearing down your black. Your black sisters and brothers...love them, encourage them, embrace them, support them. We all have a purpose in this life and I'm here to encourage you to find it with ya black ass.

My black is ________________________________
____
____.

"You are growing into consciousness, and my wish for you is that you feel no need to constrict yourself to make other people comfortable."
— Ta-Nehisi Coates, Between the World and Me

Toxic Flags On The Play

These are concepts that prohibit us from being the best versions of ourselves. They stop our growth emotionally, mentally and spiritually. More specifically, they prevent our relationships from being as fruitful as they could be. Read this in hopes of discriminating toxic bullshit from healthy shit in the present and future.

The Red Flags

/'red 'flags/ | noun

warning of danger; a sign of some particular problem requiring attention

I need you to pay attention ladies. No seriously, pay attention. Red flags are something that we as women ignore. And let me tell you why our little emotional asses ignore it... because we always see the freaking potential. But I'm here to say, fuck a potential when there are continuous red flags involved. Especially in the beginning stages of dealing with a man, friend, job, etc. Those red flags aren't there for decoration; they're there for good purposes. But of course, we overlook them because we see what it could possibly be. As women, we need to learn to focus on what we see right then and there. What we see in the beginning is ultimately what we end up getting. Yes, people do change for who and what they want, but people don't change overnight. After a few months of the draining job, you might eventually get accustomed to the toxic environment but are you willing to take the ride of the continuous ups and downs? And I know we feel that we should, but in all honesty, we shouldn't. When we start seeing the many different red flags, it means it is time for you to focus and invest in yourself. Don't ignore the red, blue, green and purple flag for "what it could possibly be." 75% of the time, it doesn't pay off in the long run. In the end, you'll only feel stupid for allowing yourself to go through all the bullshit when you knew better. If it was real and meant for you like it is supposed to be, it wouldn't be any or that many red flags. Of course, you go through things to understand the person or thing more. I'm not advising anyone to give up on someone/ something, but when the red flag turns into red flags then blue flags, then yellow flags...that's the time you need to look at your worth. Now for the other 25% of the time, it does pay off. You have some people/ things that acknowledge their own wrongdoings and actually change for the better. When that occurs, it is a true blessing, and you must not take it for granted. Verbally acknowledge their change to ensure they know they are appreciated.

In summary, only you know how much you can bear. I'm here to tell you that it doesn't take you going through hell to prove it's worth it. Stop ignoring the red flags and take heed. Do something about it now before it's too late.

"Ignoring red flags because you want to see the good in people will cost you later."- Unknown

The Heel

\ 'hēl | noun

The first or last piece of bread in a loaf

Look at you. Running around slaving in the kitchen for a guy that barely responds to your text messages. He usually texts back 2-3 hours later, but he responded right back after you asked him was he hungry. Smh. And look at you over there... killing yourself for a job that is paying you minimum wage and will replace you the same day of your funeral. Why do we do this to ourselves? Literally letting the world treat us like we are the first slice in the loaf of bread. Why are we continuously not setting the standards that we should have when this is literally our world? Ladies, we have to reclaim our time. We're doing ourselves a dishonor by not setting the bar where it should be. We accept so much bullshit thinking we are being a "strong black woman" or a "ride or die" when we are left alone to pick up the pieces of our broken selves. It's not fair and we have to stop this shit. I mean it. We are not just the first piece of bread; we are the first, middle, last AND the butter. That job that is paying you minimum wage when you are working your ass off... leave it. You have outgrown that place and you deserve more. The man that thinks he can text you at 12:30 a.m. with the eye emoji's and have you opening the door for him... ignore him. He only has 4 inches of dick and no type of conversation anyways. One of my favorite authors once stated that we settle for crumbs because we rather have a piece of them than nothing at all while we starve everyday not receiving what we need. The moment I read that, I realized that I rather not have any of it at all than lose myself chasing a piece of them. The disrespect that we have for ourselves stops now. We want therefore we will get. See you at the top sis.

"Baby girl respect is just the minimum!"
- Lauryn Hill

The Narcissist

/ˈnärsəsəst/ | noun

a person who has an excessive interest in or admiration of themselves

I would say to stay away from these types of people, but narcissists are like wolves in sheep clothing. You won't know you're even dealing with a narcissist until they are tired of wearing their mask. I read a meme online and it describes a narcissist perfectly. It basically stated that no matter the situation when dealing with a narcissist, it didn't happen. And if it did happen, it wasn't that bad. If it is that bad, they didn't mean to do it. If they meant to do it, somehow you made them do it and that there is exactly what goes through a narcissist's mindset.

Some characteristics of narcissists:

1. **They hate being alone.** The fear of rejection and seclusion makes them feel as if they are not worthy. They constantly have to be surrounded around people to feed off of. Their ego lacks when they are not getting the reassurance they feel that they deserve.

2. **They are very charming.** They are the "girl or boy next door." They always know what to say or what to do. That's because they are so calculated in their actions. They first read the room and what people like and then do exactly what they have learned. They try to make sure that people could never depict them as the "bad guy" or "bad girl."

3. **They are very manipulating.** They get a high from belittling certain situations and people. In their mind, everyone and thing is the problem and not them. They will be evil with their words and actions to make you feel a certain type of way. When they bring you down, they bring themselves up.

4. **They lack anger control.** They become outraged at just about anything. They get so angry at the fact that something or someone doesn't align with their beliefs. It threatens their ego and when angry, they are very unpredictable. Some are dangerous; some are not. You never really know until you're in an angry situation with them.

5. **They are liars**. Habitual liars at that. Most times, they lie for no reason. When they lie, they feel they are in control. The bigger the lie, the better they feel. They feel that they have won especially when they are not held accountable.

6. **They hate boundaries.** They hate feeling controlled. Why do they hate this? Because they feel that they must be in control. They want to be the leaders. They want to be the "head honcho". They want to call the shots. You are a threat to them when you try to set boundaries.

7. **They are capable of love, but can only love at their capacity.** The different levels of love vary between narcissists. It all depends on their own experiences. An important thing you must know is that they only love the things you say and do for them. They love it until they're tired of it.

8. **They only like to surround themselves around enablers and tongue biters**. Because narcissists have to have "their way," they only wish to be around people that feed their ego. The enablers will pat them on the back for all their toxic shit and the tongue biters are simply too scared to call out their shit. Narcissists love this. They feel "untouched" and "unbothered."

Narcissists cannot be "cured." There isn't a type of medicine you can take if you are diagnosed with a narcissistic personality disorder. Narcissists can only learn how to cope with their disorder. How do they do this? Therapy. Learning what first caused narcissism to come about and being aware of their actions while navigating through life.

When you are in a relationship with a narcissist, things initially are great. Do you know why? Because they do everything that they feel you would want and desire. They either have learned this from their previous relationship or have studied you. A famous youtuber calls it the "love bomb" stage. Everything is literally perfect, from what they say to what they do. They feel as though they have to give you everything in the beginning, so when you find out who they really are, you'll be more pronged to staying around. Things change when they slowly start to show their true character and you are not as accepting. That's when they begin to stop all those little things that they were once doing and create themselves to be the victim. From there, the manipulation, lies, and everything else starts. At that point, leave. Get out of that relationship. They will literally drive you to the point of depression. Leave and seek help from a therapist. It hurts, but at that point, you have to take care of yourself and understand that a narcissist will never change; they'll only move on to find their next victim.

"Aye, time is extremely valuable and I prefer to waste it on girls that's basic. That's just some Ye' shit."-Kanye West

Side Chick

/sīd CHik/ | noun

a mistress; a woman one dates in addition to one's girlfriend or wife, usually in secret

It's not where he's at; it's where he wants to be huh? Sis, it was only cool for Keyshia Cole to say it. I promise you if he wanted to be there, he would. I'm not here to judge because we all have been side chicks before, whether it was knowingly or unknowingly. When I was one knowingly, I thought I had it going on. At the time, I thought I was on top of the world. He was feeding me, giving me money, spending time with me, validating my feelings and I was with him more than the freaking girlfriend. I thought I was the chosen one. Boy, was I wrong. When he would be with me and answer her call, I felt so small inside. I would get mad, and he would say, "Stop tripping baby, I just don't want to hear her mouth." I would say okay, but in reality... I was hurt. Why in the hell was I hurt though? This man didn't owe me any loyalty at all. I was just sex and a nice catch in his eyes. The truth of the matter was that I was insecure, and I didn't love myself. Not enough anyways. I couldn't have if I was accepting the absolute bare minimum. Ladies, I'm sorry to tell you that you don't love yourself that much either if you are accepting to only be his side chick. I mean, why aren't you enough to be his main girlfriend? Don't feed me that "Oh, I don't want him to be my boyfriend, I only want what he can give me." Well damn! What can he give you that you can't give yourself? Oh yeah, penis. Girl, if you don't buy you a toy or use your little fingers until you find a man that will recognize your worth. You will find a man, but build yourself up first before you go exploring in this evil world. Being a side chick just isn't worth the embarrassment and loss of self-respect.

Now to my ladies that was unknowingly the side chicks. Been there, done that. After you find out, you start questioning every single detail that he once told you. Now you're like damn, how was I that stupid not to know? You weren't "that stupid." You were just living in the moment. Sometimes we get so caught up focusing on the good, that we can't even see the bad. Don't even trip. His karma will come back. Now the biggest question I have for you is, whenever you did find out, did you stay? Did you pick fights with the main girl? Did you try to fight him? What did you do? I know you were hurt and embarrassed so I'm curious to know. When I found out I was a side chick, I was a snitch. I felt obligated to share the story with the main. Not to be funny or messy, but I was like, "Girl this nigga tried to play us like some dummies?" Can y'all believe she thought I was lying and wanted to start drama with me? I was shocked. I still can't believe women are really that oblivious. It happened so long ago, but I honestly believe I just left him and her alone. Did he leave me alone? No! I had to ghost him. Did he ever change for her? No! Are they still together? I think so, but God bless their souls because I know sis is catching hell...still. Look at all the turmoil that one small role can cause. It's way too much unwanted confusion. Just say no to the whole idea of being a side chick. It's not worth it. I promise it's not.

"If he ain't gonna' love you the way he should, then let it go."- Keyshia Cole

Changed Places

/chānj plās/ | verb

to give a different position, course, or direction to

Here's some tissue sis. Wipe your face. I know how you feel. They're just not the same anymore. They changed places. Yes, it hurts but what are you supposed to do? Sit and cry all day while they continue to live their best life? Stop that shit. You're better than that. Yes, your feelings are valid. Yes, you do matter. Yes, I feel you. I swear I really do. But life goes on and eventually, the hurt that you're feeling will fade. I know you sit and drive and have flashbacks of the way things used to be. You used to be so happy, and you felt like you were on top of the world. It seems like yesterday huh? The days y'all would look each other in the eye and have no worries about who, what, when, where or why. All that mattered was them and that moment. They were your morning and your night. You were willing to do whatever, whenever, however, weren't you? I know you were and I'm not mad at you. You did all of that because you thought that was your "person," that's why. Don't beat yourself up. You were giving unconditional love, that's all. Unconditional love is something that is very rare. Most people in this generation don't receive nor even give unconditional love without any regard. So honestly, it's their loss sis. Now wipe your tears. No. You know what? Fuck that; I changed my mind. Cry! And cry again. And if you want to cry again, then so be it. You deserve that shit and don't let no one make you feel different.

Damn right, you're pressed about it. Don't try to hide it. And don't try to cope with it through drugs or sex. Allow yourself to feel the pain. Grieve the pain now. Give yourself a time limit whether it is 2 weeks, a month, two months, or whatever. And when that time limit is up, that is when I want you to wipe your tears because best believe, we have moves to make. One monkey don't stop a show. They showed who they were, so it's time to let go of the "what if's." There aren't anymore. Focus on the present and what actually happened. The unfortunate truth of the matter is that they changed places. They're no longer in your corner. They're somewhere around the block or probably with that... girl. (I had to choose my language wisely). And don't stress yourself out about her sis. It looks like glitz and glamour on the outside, but in reality... they're damaged and until they heal their spirit and mind, they will tear down every female as well as themselves. Let karma do its due diligence. What we need to focus on is you, your healing and your future. Focus on what things will look like for you in the next month or year. Focus on making sure those babies of yours are passing their classes. Focus on that dream house that you've been talking about for the longest. Focus on your credit score. Make sure that it goes up 50 points like you want it to.

One thing that I want you to understand is that the human brain is a complex body part that one cannot operate without. Within the inner brain, there is something called the hypothalamus. It's small but carries out many functions within the body. It controls behaviors such as hunger, thirst, sleep, and sexual response. It also regulates body temperature, blood pressure, emotions, and the secretion of hormones. The female hypothalamus is twice as large as the males. Therefore, we biologically tend to be more emotionally invested than them. You're wondering how they can possibly act as if "they don't care" as much as you do when things changed, and one possible answer is simply because they can't. They don't have the capacity to feel something as you do. I'm not making any excuses for their nonchalant behavior, but this is one possible answer. Stop working yourself up about something you don't have control over. They changed places and that's just that.

"You went from my biggest fan to my biggest hater."- Young Dolph

To The Person I Planned My Life With

\ 'eks\ | Noun

a former spouse or former partner in an intimate relationship

You really had me going. I'm not going to be like the rest of society and act like I'm not hurt. I'm going to be completely honest with you and say I am beyond hurt. I can't even begin to describe the way that I'm feeling. You were my person. My go-to. My best friend. We shared everything together and most importantly, we planned our life together. We planned it down from the house, our kid's names, and our future career plans. What happened? I thought you loved me? Love doesn't hurt. Not like this. I was willing to weather any storm with you, but you became my biggest storm to weather. I remember the day when I first told you I was in love with you. We laid in bed and I started crying. You wiped my tears and you asked me what was wrong. I could barely breathe at the time. You hugged me and kept asking me what was wrong. I told you I was afraid. You asked me what I was afraid of. I said, "I'm afraid because I'm in love with you and it's nothing I can do about it." You looked me in my eyes, and you said you loved me and that you would never let me go... but you did. This world was wicked and you let this world corrupt you. What happened? What happened to all the promises we made? You made! What happened to the smile you once had? What happened to your innocent spirit? I don't see it anymore and I honestly don't know if I'll ever see it again. It hurts for me to face the fact. You were my person. You're just not my person anymore.

Ladies, I believe we've all planned our lives with a certain person, or maybe even multiple people. We weren't wrong for looking towards the future with any of them. We had faith in them and the relationship. It's nothing wrong with that. Just don't lose faith in love. Maybe the person you planned your life with just wasn't the person you were supposed to spend the rest of your life with. That's okay. Maybe you were supposed to gain something from that relationship. Let's focus on that. You must let go of that life you once planned and start looking to build a new one. It doesn't necessarily have to be a life with another person, but right now, let's focus on the life you are planning with yourself.

I once planned my life with ____________, but now I'm working on planning my life with ______ (insert your name).

Going Forward (Healing From the Toxicity)

This section focuses on the importance of looking forward. It's concepts at random that will help us heal. We can show up and out in our careers, friendships, relationships and personal encounters just by mastering and learning something from these concepts. We have done the work already by looking at our past and present, so now let's take time to look toward our future.

Closure

/'klōZHər/ | noun

the summary or explanation of what has happened prior to the transition of something new

I gave you the book definition, but I want you to ask yourself... what exactly is this thing called closure? In my eyes, it's a hoax. A real life scam. It's something that we long for so that we don't feel bad for the situation that we were put in. It's what we secretly desire because we don't want that person to be the monster that they showed they really are. Why long for closure when the disrespect itself was the closure? They showed you who and what they were. Why are we still asking for more? Believe them. I remember in college, I was talking to a guy and he "ghosted" me out of nowhere. Me and him were intimately involved in a long-distance situationship for about 6-8 months. We would go on baecations, I met his family and friends, we went out on dates, we stayed on the phone all night, we told each other "I love you" ... I mean, we were basically in a relationship just not exclusively (Toxic right? Yeah, I know). The problem was... he had everything going for himself, but potential (COMPLETE RED FLAG). He was so comfortable where he was, and I was not. From his job, school, friends, everything. It was so draining trying to force him to be better, but I believed in him and didn't want to give up on him.

One morning, I woke up to a good morning text and I responded back like normal. 10 minutes passed, then 30, then 2 hours, then 5 hours, then 10, then 15, then the next day came, then it turned into 2 days, then a whole week, then 3 weeks, then a month. All throughout that time, I was sending essays, calling his phone from different numbers, writing him on social media and trying to find his mom's number. Hell, I even thought about pulling up to his mom's house. I was just trying to figure out what happened. I initially thought his phone was off because he would always "forget to pay the bill." Then I thought he was in a car wreck or something. I made every excuse in the world. It wasn't until a week later that I realized he ghosted me because it showed that he was active on Instagram 5 minutes after I checked. Even still, I was still blowing him up because I wanted some damn answers! I wanted "closure." I was so confused about what happened and why he felt the need to ignore me when I did nothing. Well actually, I did everything. I was patient and there for him to figure out his bullshit. Do you know that a month and a half later, he texted me an essay apologizing for going ghost? He told me he had realized that he wasn't enough for me, and he was ashamed. I honestly don't even think I texted back because I was like WTF. At that point, I was over it. I didn't care what excuse he had because as a friend and man, he had an obligation to just be transparent. Still to this day, he hearts my picture and tries to shoot me those "You look good. Hope all is well" texts. Funny right? But now that I look back, I'm embarrassed. I'm embarrassed because I went on for weeks trying to find closure when I knew he wasn't shit. I mean, I knew it from the jump. I wrote all those essays and did all the stalking and calling for absolutely nothing. It's like I knew he wasn't shit, but I wanted him to tell me he wasn't shit. Although I knew I was nothing but a good friend to him and he had no reason to treat me the way he did, I wanted him to say it. But why? He had already shown me. The disrespect itself was enough closure, so why did I disrespect myself even more trying to pull his teeth to get "closure." Even when he did text me back a month and a half later and gave me the "closure" I had begged for, it didn't even mean anything. I still had questions and a comeback, so even if he had said it earlier, it wouldn't have meant anything.

Since then, I realized that closure means nothing. It's a fake toxic hoax. Ladies, I know you want to know the answers... but you know it already. If it looks like a duck, quack like a duck and walk like a duck... guess what it is? A freaking duck. Step into your standards and stop allowing the disrespect to continue. Stop the long essay messages. Stop calling from fake numbers. Stop writing subliminal messages on social media. Just stop. It's not worth it. But guess what is worth it? You are. You are the bag sis, so act like it.

*I no longer need closure from*__________________
____
____
____
____
____.

GVO

/good vahybz'ōnlē/ | noun

a slang/ phrase for the positive feelings given off by a person, place, or situation

"*It's a vibe, it's a vibe. It's a vibe.*" Okay I'm sorry, but that song by 2 Chainz and Jhene Aiko is literally a vibe. Listen, ladies if I could scream this, I would. PROTECT YOUR ENERGY! Let me say it again for the people in the back, PROTECT YOUR ENERGY. Wait a minute, let me be a little louder for my sisters that's purposely trying to miss this message... PROTECT YOUR ENERGY. Sometimes people are battling so many demons of their own that they reflect that energy on you. And it's not fair. I mean, why do you have to be attacked during "girl's night" with condescending remarks simply because their boyfriend cheated on them? The answer to that is, you don't. That's not your battle to fight. But let me warn you, as soon as you don't react the way they want you to, everything you do is coming off as "doing too much" or "you think that you're better than them" or "you don't even care." Y'all must hit them with my best friend's favorite line,

"Be Blessed." Because baby, they are fighting demons that you should not be in the business of trying to get in the ring with.

Walk into a room knowing you bring nothing but good energy. I get it; you just got a text saying your credit score dropped right before you walked into the door, but how do you know that the next person you speak to didn't just find out that they have Chlamydia? You have to be nice to people. Bring good energy and good vibes only. Life is hard enough man.

I also want to add that when you sense bad energy, it is perfectly okay to eliminate yourself. Unfortunately, everyone doesn't have good vibes and we don't have to force ourselves to be around that. People love to scream, "Oh she mad," "She hatin," "She thinks she better than us." NO! Maybe she just doesn't want to be around the energy that you all bring. Forget what they say; it's not about them. It's solely about you and your mental capacity. So, if you need to unfollow on social media, block them from your phone, pretend you're on the phone when you see them walking towards you or even miss out on an event, DO THAT. Gravitate towards good vibes and good vibes only.

Walk into a room bringing the energy that everyone can feel.

Close The Door

/ klōz(d)'dôr/ | adjective

a door that is shut

I know it may be frightening, but sometimes it's necessary for us to close the door. We need to close it to block everything else out and focus on us. We have to learn how to be okay by ourselves. Stop running from yourself. Give yourself a chance. You don't always have to pick up the phone to call someone or try to invite someone over. Learn how to be okay with being alone. When we value being alone, we value our peace. Stop trying to figure yourself out through a man, club or a friend. It can all be so simple as utilizing a Saturday and doing everything you love right by yourself. Start yourself off with a 15-minute workout, cook yourself some breakfast, take a shower, find a good series on Netflix, take a nap and order a pizza. Scroll on social media here and there and just enjoy your own company. If you want to get cute and take selfies, do that. Put on a good playlist while you're getting dolled up and just vibe with yourself. Master who you are. Embrace it. Embrace that small booty while you're dancing to City Girls. Embrace your nappy coals while you're slicking those edges down. Close the damn door and celebrate you. When we celebrate ourselves, it's not a soul or thing that can rain on our parade.

When I mastered the beauty of enjoying myself, I stopped caring about sleeping alone in the bed or if someone called me back. I no longer cared about the flakey friends or the stupid events that was so "lit" that I missed. I realized that I just did not have the energy to waste on any of those petty things. I grasped that I was a damn good catch right by myself and I didn't need anyone or thing to validate me or my characteristics. Trust me when I say you're not missing out on anything when you're getting shit together. I strongly advise you to close the door and get YOU together; it'll be worth it.

Recharge and revamp!

Self- Care

/ self-luhv /| noun

the instinct by which one's actions are directed to the promotion of one's own welfare or well-being, especially an excessive regard for one's own advantage

The sweetest thing I've ever known. So pure. So precious. So necessary. One thing that my therapist always tells me is *"Self-Care Isn't Selfish"* and we as individuals must believe that. As women, we have so many responsibilities to fulfill, like taking care of the kids, meeting hour requirements at work, making sure that our mom's health is in good shape, trying to clean the house, budgeting our finances, checking in on our friends, passing our classes in school, etc., that we forget about us. We neglect our own mental and overall wellbeing to make sure that everyone else and thing is taken care of. But that's a generational curse from our ancestors. Let me clarify that statement by saying that although it is a blessing to have the strength and resiliency that our ancestors had, we feel obligated to continue to let our torches burn without ever blowing the torch out. So, this section here is encouraging you to take care of yourself. There is no book definition of what self-care looks like because it differs for everyone. It doesn't always have to be a spa day because it may look like you lying in bed doing nothing but watching Netflix all day. Self-care is whatever makes you feel good and brings you a sense of peace. I personally enjoy traveling, brunching with my girlfriends, lying in bed doing nothing, hiring cleaning ladies to help with my house, attending monthly therapy sessions with my therapist, listening to Jhene Aiko and Brent Faiyaz, not drinking sodas and limiting myself on social media. That's a few to name, but definitely some that I recommend you try. I know you are a boss and I know there are "no days off," but if you keep thinking that… you will be forced to have days off. We are not robots. We are not trained to keep going and going and going. We need sleep. We need breaks. We need rest and we need it all on the regular. Stop cheating yourself.

So, I challenge you to write down at least 4 things that you will engage in every month for yourself. Remember, self-care isn't selfish.

1. ______________________________________

2. ______________________________________

3. ______________________________________

4. ______________________________________

It's personal!

Coping

/koh-ping/ | noun

to face and deal with responsibilities, problems, or difficulties, especially successfully or in a calm or adequate manner

Coping is a fancy word for "taking care of yourself." It sounds simple, but at times it can be extremely hard to cope when you're in frustrating situations. Coping needs to take place when you are facing feelings of anger, frustration, sadness, disappointment, stress and fear. Taking some extra steps to cope and decrease your overall tension can prevent your feelings from spiraling out of control.

Tips for coping by MHA Screening:

1. **Pause before reacting to the problem/ situation.** Take a deep breath, count to 10, take an hour or two, walk away. Just simply pause. When you give yourself that pause, you can properly evaluate and respond. When we don't give ourselves that proper break, we sometimes overreact to the problem/situation.

2. **Change your surroundings.** Physically relocating yourself can help you begin to calm down. Go to another room or step outside for a few minutes of fresh air to help disrupt the track that your mind is on.

3. **Release built up energy**. Exercise is a great way to get rid of extra energy and can improve your mood. Some people find grounding exercises (like meditation or deep breathing) helpful to calm intense feelings, while others prefer more high-impact activities like running or weightlifting. Think about what you usually do to decompress, like taking a hot shower or blasting your favorite music and use the tools that you know work for you.

4. **Eliminate the stressors.** Sometimes there's no way to completely get rid of a big problem, but there's often more than just one issue contributing to your frustration. Things like an overwhelming workload or unhealthy relationships can make you feel on edge. Pay attention to how and why you're feeling stressed and see if you can make small changes to improve a challenging situation to make it less burdensome.

5. **Get organized.** Dedicate a few minutes each day to tidying, planning, or reorganizing. Implementing a routine can also help you feel more on top of things by adding structure and certainty to your daily life.

6. **Manage your expectations.** Negative feelings often stem from people or situations not meeting your standards or assumptions. It's frustrating to feel let down, but recognize that you can't fully predict anyone else's behavior or how situations will play out. Shift your mental framework so that you aren't setting yourself up for disappointment.

7. **Seek help.** If you feel that you can't control things on your own, it's okay to get extra support. Things can feel explosive if you don't. Reach out to mental health professionals if necessary.

Proprietary data. MHAScreening.org. 2020. Ibid. IBM Watson Health-NPR Health Poll. November 1-14, 2018. https://www.ibm.com/downloads/cas/2YQ8NLD5

Therapy

/THerəpē/ | noun

the treatment of mental or psychological disorders by psychological means

T-h-e-r-a-p-y. A topic that's so underrated, especially within the black community. When having problems within the average black household, we are told to keep our faith and trust God. Which as a firm believer in Christ, I am not taking anything from. But without the work... our faith means nothing. That is exactly what therapy is; it's work. Hard work actually. It's not a place that you go to simply talk about your problems. It's a place you go to work through your problems. It's a big difference. It's a nonjudgmental zone, where legally, your therapist cannot share anything that is discussed unless you state you are going to harm yourself, someone else or if you claim someone else is planning to harm you. It's a place where you can be completely vulnerable. People always say, "Why do I need a therapist when I can just call my best friend Aliyah for free?" You need a therapist because you don't have to worry about your therapist showing up to your cookout and looking at the person whom you shared raped you when you were 5 years old. Or you don't have to feel judged when you share you decided to go back to your abusive boyfriend for the 10th time. Nor do you have to worry about you all falling out and them sharing all your personal business. You will be working with a trained individual that will not be biased regardless of what you share. They won't encourage you to keep talking with your toxic mom simply because they are your mom. They won't try to convince you to stay at a job that is not healthy for you. They will give you the unbiased complete truth. They will help you uncover layers of hurt that you probably didn't even know was there. I remember when I was talking with my therapist about the arguments I was having with my ex-boyfriend always leaving the house. She listened to me and then looked me in my eyes and said, "What was your relationship like with your dad? Tell me about him." I was so frustrated and in defense, I started screaming at her. I asked "What does this have to do with my dad? My dad was great. I'm talking about my boyfriend." She asked me again to tell me about him. I told her and described him in detail, from his personality to the type of shoes he likes to wear. She then asked me to tell her my feelings regarding him and my mom's relationship. Woah. I always had certain feelings about them, but it was very rare that I spoke out loud about their relationship. We dug deep into their relationship and she then asked, "Have you ever felt abandoned?" I cried a river. I cried because damn right, I have. You know how hard it is to see your parents' relationship suffer due to adultery. I now know and accept that their personal choices had nothing to do with me, but for so long, I didn't feel like that. I always wondered why our family wasn't good enough. Most importantly, I wondered why I wasn't a good enough daughter to want them to do right for each other and just love on our family. It wasn't until I had a conversation with my therapist that I realized that I was carrying my childhood abandonment issues and insecurities into my relationship. It was like I finally understood a part of me that I never knew existed. It really wasn't wrong that my boyfriend wanted to go out from time to time and it wasn't fair for me to make him feel bad, but I did. I was wrong. I give thanks to my therapist because prior to our discussion I went through life thinking everyone else was the problem, but really it was me and my own childhood issues. Therapy has the power to do that. Therapy is so necessary and so needed. Don't just take it from me; go find out yourself. Do yourself a favor.

Resources:

www. Therapyforblackgirls.com

www. Goodtherapy.org

psychologytoday.com

Safe Place

/sāf plās/| noun

a place intended to be free of bias, conflict, criticism, or potentially threatening actions, ideas, or conversations

I'm curious to know where/ what is your safe place? Where do you feel most comfortable and vulnerable? Where do you let your hair down? After a long day, where do you know you can go and automatically feel relieved? What is the one place where nothing or one else matters? Where can you get the worst absolute news but are able to process the information in one of the healthiest ways simply because you are there? Where is it the place you have cried until you couldn't cry anymore and did not feel embarrassed? I mean, I'm really curious. Is it your bedroom? Your bathroom? Your man's arms? Your back porch? Your car? The beauty salon? The nail salon? Your therapist's office? Your doctor's office? Your sunroom? Your best friend's house? Your mom's house? The park? The beach? The parking lot of a mall? The back seat of an uber? Or do you not have one? If you don't have one, get one. It doesn't have to be anywhere fancy, but it needs to be a place where you can get peace of mind. If you do have one, then how often do you go? Once a month? Once a week? Every day? I can't tell you how or when you should go because I don't know your routine, but I try to go to my place daily. I need it though. With all the hectic drama that I hear and go through, I need my peace of mind. I don't care what else my day consists of; I make sure that my safe place is a part of my routine. We neglect so many things that we know are healthy for us like eating vegetables, drinking water and exercising daily, but why? It's time to stop neglecting our minds, bodies and souls. It's time to do the necessary work. Dedicate yourself to find a safe place. It's time for new beginnings. You'll thank yourself in the long end.

My safe place is ______________________________

____

____

____

____.

Mentor

/ˈmen͵tôr/ | noun

an experienced and trusted adviser

"It's not what you know, it's who you know." Growing up, I thought that was the stupidest thing ever to say. In my head, I always thought if I was smart and did the hard work, why would it be about who I know? It wasn't until I was in college that I learned to work smarter, not harder. As women, it's so hard to network and take criticism from others how we should, but I'm here to tell you to go out and network. Find and connect with someone that you feel can water your grass. It's okay to follow to learn how to lead. Personally, I don't just have one mentor. I have a mentor for every area that I wish to seek growth in. I present my own ideas to them and ask for their personal and professional opinion. It's just a simple torch passing ordeal. Why reinvent the wheel? There are hundreds and thousands of people that understand exactly where you are in life and won't mind sharing the tea. Don't be afraid, go after it. It can all be as simple as a DM. You miss all the shots that you don't take.

To my mentors, thank you for always being an open book. Thank you for challenging me when I needed it. It is and always will be most appreciated.

Megan thee Stallion VS Michelle Obama

Megan thee Stallion, a hot female rapper, was born and raised in the South Park neighborhood of Houston. She has hit records such as "Big Ole Freak" and "WAP". She advocates for self-confidence through explicit raps and dances.

Michelle Obama is the wife of 44th U.S. president Barack Obama. She served as the first African American lady from 2009-2017. As an ivy league graduate, she serves as a mother, a fashion icon and role models to many individuals.

Once upon a time, I saw a meme and I don't know if it was a shade attempt or not, but it was saying how women portray to be "Michelle Obama," but are "Megan the Stallions" in real life. The meme had me puzzled. I really think it was meant to be "shade," but it was literally nothing but stupidity. Who said that we can't be both? Life is all about balance. It's important to be multidimensional. If I want to twerk and drink Dusse' on Saturday night with my girlfriends, and then on Monday give a presentation to my cohort at school while having a cup of coffee, then so what? If I'm being responsible and having clean fun, what is the problem? At least I'm not portraying to be the holiest child of God, but out here being a homewrecker... OOOPPPPS! Did I say that? Now THAT my sister is when you're not living in your truth. I'm a person of many dimensions and most of all, I love to enjoy my life. Life is extremely too short not to enjoy. I work hard as fuck. I deserve a break and I don't care whose daughter or son is mad about it and neither should you.

Ladies, don't let these miserable people guilt trip you for being a Megan the Stallion and Michelle Obama. Because guess what? They both are successful black women at the end of the day. Yes, they have different routes to their success, but don't we all? I don't see anything wrong with it and it's not a soul that will be able to tell me different. So cheers to all my Megan's and Michelle's! WE UP SISTERS! #RHGS

"When they go low, we go high!"
– Michelle Obama

"I'm a hot girl, I do hot shit!"
- Megan The Stallion

Howard University

\ 'hau̇(-ə)rd ˌyü-nə-'vər-sə-tē\ | noun

A private, federally charted historical black college university was founded on March 2, 1867, in Washington, DC. It offers undergraduate, graduate, and professional degrees in more than 120 programs. It is deemed as the #1 HBCU in the world.

HHHHHHHH...UUUUUU.. You know! My dearest Howard University. Howard was one of the greatest things that happened to me, and I say that in the humblest way. It was the place that made me a better me. I always joke and tell people that I'm from DC because I feel that DC is the place that made me who I am now. I left home when I was 17 years old and I learned more about myself at Howard than I learned within my 17 years of life. Sometimes when we are in familiar places and around people that make us feel comfortable, we get complacent. We become stuck in our same everyday routines. We eat the same foods, go to the same hang-out places, see the same people, have the same arguments with our friends, shop at the same stores, over and over again. We are made to believe that whatever is accepted by our family and childhood friends is the only way of life. Let me explicitly say that it's nothing wrong with being comfortable with your family and friends, but you have to ask yourself... how will you ever grow if you're not challenged?

I knew it was time for me to leave South Carolina because I no longer felt challenged. I'm not saying that to brag, but I'm being completely honest. I had accomplished my goals of being president of my elementary, middle and high school class, graduated with honors, became involved with every club I could think of (drama, spanish, beta, debate, etc.), received my license and got my first car, had my dose of the high school sweetheart love, was on the cheerleading team... I mean the list could go on. I was deemed "popular," and yes, it was fun, but it became stressful and boring. It became stressful because I could never let my guard down because everyone knew me. I felt like I had to be dressed in the latest Rocawear outfits with my hair done simply because I was known for that. It became boring because I did the same routines, literally. But Howard... it was the complete opposite. It was a place where no one knew me, and I had the chance to recreate who I wanted to be. There was not a preconceived notion of who or what I should be like. I no longer had to be in a box. I had the chance to start over.

My friends weren't just telling me what I wanted to hear to keep me as a friend, but they were telling me what I needed to hear because they genuinely wanted to be my friend. My professors weren't trying to pass me and sugar-coat anything because they knew my family; they gave me the raw uncut truth. I wish I could share my experience in detail and one day, I think I will. The purpose of this section is for you to answer, "What is/was your Howard University?" What is the one place, thing, job, etc., that you experienced that made you grow? What made you step out of your comfort zone and look at life in a completely different way? And if you can't think of anything, what do you think it can be? I once read, "We miss all the shots that we don' take." And that is the absolute truth. We can't be afraid to take risks because those same risks could be the risks that change our life. Stop cutting corners and prepare yourself for change. So again, I ask you, what was/is your Howard University?

My Howard University is ________________.

"She went to Howard, her head strong, her mamma tall, so her legs long. She went to college and got her masters, now she bringing that bread home." – The Game

Give it a break

/brāk/ | noun

a pause in work or during an activity or event

Stop that shit. Stop arguing. Stop sending long texts. Stop making subliminal posts on social media. Stop blaming yourself. Stop wishing bad on others. Stop going live and cursing, making a fool out of yourself. Stop going out trying to keep yourself busy. Stop spending money that you know you should be saving. Stop popping pills knowing that you're killing yourself. Stop thinking of more things to say and calling them back. Stop taking your anger out on your sister, knowing you're only mad at one person. Stop calling out of work saying you're dealing with a "family emergency," knowing you need to go to work and make some money. Stop thinking about bullshit while you're driving, causing yourself to get a speeding ticket. Stop lying about the situation, trying to make the other person look like the villain. Stop downplaying everything about someone. Stop spreading rumors. Stop having sex with all these different partners trying to fill a void that you will probably never be able to fill.

Just stop girl. Stop and give it a break right now. Can you do that for me? You have already done enough. Do you know all the wasted energy that you're devoting to a dead situation? Do you realize what you could be doing instead of plotting on someone else's downfall? I'm not saying your feelings aren't valid. Whether you're dealing with a best friend's betrayal or a heartbreak. I feel you. The shit is painful and stressful. But you have to give it a break for now and trust that God will deliver your steps and most of all, handle the situation. Trust me, things will work out just like it's supposed to.

I am giving ______________________________

____

________________________________ *a break.*

Leaving the Relationship

/lēv/ | verb

ending a previous relationship that you were once intimately involved in

"*Na-na-na-na Na-na-na-na, Hey! Hey! Hey! Goodbyeeeee!*" I'm honestly playing. I had to start off by bringing some humor into this section. Leaving a relationship is so freaking hard. No matter if it was 5 months, 10 months, 2 years or 10 years. It's hard. Why? Because during the time frame y'all were together, they became "your person." The person you first wake up to talk to. The person you go to for sound advice. The person you enjoy most of your days with. The person you value. The person you love. In the earlier section, we discussed the process of grieving a relationship. For now, I want to remind you that when you lose a relationship... don't lose yourself too. Use that time that to focus on yourself. Figure out what exactly went wrong on your end. Regardless if you feel like it was your fault that the relationship ended, look yourself in the mirror and ask yourself, "What could I have done better?" You do this not to guilt-trip yourself but to make yourself better for the relationship you are destined to be in. It's going to hurt, bad at that. It's expected, but don't give up on yourself or love. Everything happens for a reason, you'll see.

Do's when you leave a relationship

1. **Remove old pictures and memories from your possession and social media sites.** It's no longer about y'all. It's about you. Keep the memories in a safe place, but replace them with pictures and memories of you and who you were before you were in the relationship.

2. **Rely on your family and friends for support.** If it was a serious relationship, you are going to need some support. You will begin the grieving process and you will need your loved ones to help you cope and vent. Although you will be the one doing most of the work, you can't do it alone.

3. **Find a new daily routine**. Your old routine probably consisted of your ex. Now that they are out of the picture, you're going to have to find one that doesn't consist of them. Make sure your new routine feeds your mind, body and spirit. With the mind piece, find a therapist or trusted loved one to help you mentally prepare yourself for your new beginning. With the body piece, figure out a workout routine that is at least 15 minutes a day. My therapist recommended that I start a work-

out routine to help start my day off on a positive note. Find a routine that works for you though. Whether it's a small routine watching a YouTube video before you go to bed or going walking during your lunch break. Spiritually, you will need to rely on whatever faith source you have. That may look like praying, going to church, reading the bible, listening to podcasts, etc. Draw closer to your religion to fill you spiritually.

4. **Write out your goals for your new beginning**. You have a fresh start to life so take advantage. You need to physically write down your goals of what you want to accomplish within the next 6 months, year and the next 5 years. Write it and place it somewhere that you can see every day. When you see your goals, speak them out loud. Manifest it and believe it.

5. **Be gentle with yourself**. This isn't a rushed process, and you shouldn't be hard on yourself. Take how much ever time you need and be strategic with everything you do.

6. **Give yourself a deadline of when you will stop living in the fantasy of you two.** It doesn't have to be sudden, but you must do it. If you continuously try to live in the past, you will block your future blessings.

Don'ts when you leave a relationship

1. **Do not go on a bashing spree or seek revenge.** You will look like the bitter one. Regardless if you are bitter or not, let karma work it's magic. I promise karma will do everything that you want to do and more. It's no need to get your hands dirty within the process. People will eventually see their true colors for what they really are.

2. **Do not try to hop into a new relationship to get over them.** Yes. Have your fun, but don't be a sucker. You should be trying to focus on yourself and your own happiness, not trying to fill the void and focus on someone else. When you try hopping into a new relationship right afterwards, you are only setting yourself up for failure. Don't waste any more time. Take it slow. It's not a race.

3. **Do not result to drugs and partying.** Although drugs and partying are a form of coping, it's unhealthy coping mechanisms. Find new habits and routines that are healthy and will benefit you in the long run.

4. **Do not think that life is over.** The only thing that is over is the relationship. Life is just now beginning for you. Take advantage of it.

5. **Do not stalk them or the "new victim."** Let them live in peace. The urge will come to see what their day consists of but fight that urge.

Whatever they do is no longer your business. Stalking them and the next victim will only make you bitter and possibly even depressed.

6. **Do not try to keep getting closure from the relationship**. You all ended for a reason and that is all the closure you need. You don't have to avoid them, but don't fall into the trap of continuously running back to hear the sorry's or to even say you're sorry. Be responsible for your own feelings. Do not expect anything from them.

"I love you, but I love myself more"- SamJ

From Hurting to Healing

/hərtiNG/ to /ˈhēliNG/ | noun

from the mental pain or distress of a person or their feelings to the process of making or becoming sound or healthy again

I know we have all been hurt by something, whether it was a best friend's betrayal, a family member passing away, being fired on your job, your boyfriend cheating on you, etc. The most beautiful thing about hurting is that healing is what comes afterwards. One important fact about healing is that you are no longer who you once were. You become a completely new person. You become this new person because who you once were is not a fit for the life you were destined to live. The old you was good for a season, but you heal and become this new person for a reason. In the beginning, the new person you become is a little... frightening. It's the person you are yet to see when you look in the mirror because all you saw was your old self. I'm here to tell you not to be afraid because that final feeling of healing is so refreshing. It's what once broke you, may still slightly ache, but it doesn't hurt as bad. Why doesn't it hurt as bad? Because you are no longer in that phase. You've grown into this new person where that phase of your life is simply JUST a phase.

Healing is not an easy process though. You endure a great sense of pain before you enjoy the beauty of healing. You have days where you can't even find the energy to get out the bed, eat, talk or even crack a smile. I remember I was hurting so bad that I didn't eat for 4 days and when I ate on the 5th day, I threw up everything. It wasn't that I was starving myself; I just could not find the energy to consume any food. I prayed to God to help me heal. I cried out to him every hour. I will admit that I was honestly mad at God because I could not understand why he would cause me to hurt this bad. I knew I was a good person, so I couldn't understand why I was put through so much pain. Similar to grieving, you have to take your time when you are healing. You must rely on your coping skills and have faith that you will make it through. We have all been there before, so don't beat yourself up or feel embarrassed; embrace your hurt because what is soon to come will be better than anything you previously had.

Tips for healing:

1. *Process your thoughts*
2. *Connect with other people*
3. *Don't compare your experience to other's*
4. *Take care of your body*
5. *Know it will take time*
6. *Give yourself grace*
7. *Don't be afraid to seek help*

"Me, myself and I. That's all I got in the end. That's what I found out. And it ain't no need to cry. I took a vow that from now on I'm gonna be my own bestfriend." - Beyonce

To The Person I Will Spend My Life With

/ ˈsōl ˌmāt/ | noun

a person ideally suited to another as a close friend or romantic partner

I've been waiting so long for you. I'm going to try my best to verbalize how deeply I feel about you. It would be simpler to say I love you, but I want to go deeper. I love the way you make me feel when I'm looking into your eyes. You make me feel heard and understood. You make me feel safe. You make me feel like nothing else matters but you and me. I waited so long for this patient and gentle love. You knew I was new to this, and you loved me through each new phase. When I am wrong, it isn't an argument... it is a discussion. When I am vulnerable, you make me feel safe with your every word and touch. When I am hurt, you are my healer. When I am happy, you are my cheerleader, just as happy as I am. When it's a problem, it's always me and you against the problem, never me and you against each other.

You make life so much easier. I used to cry and pray to God to send me someone to share my life with, and he outdid himself when he sent me you. I am so grateful. I can't let go. I won't let go. I promise. I made a promise to be here, but I'm not promising that everything will be easy. Life is hard and the devil attacks what he can't get, so I'm sure it'll be hard. But this right here that I want to give you... it's called unconditional love. That means in any circumstance at any place; I will love you under all and any conditions. Thank you for being you. I can't wait to spend the rest of my life with you.

Love you with all my heart. SamJ.

A prayer to you,

Dear heavenly Father, I come to you as humbly as I can to first say thank you. Thank you for life, health and strength. Thank you for the breath in our body and the means to walk, talk, think and act. Dear Lord, I pray You cover every individual that found the time to read this prayer. Heal their mind, body and souls. Change their negative thoughts to more positive thoughts. Change their negative acts to more constructive acts. Lord, I'm not asking for perfection, but only for guidance to the life that you see fit for us. I pray that at least one message, paragraph, sentence and or quote resonated with someone. I pray that we all understand that we are not alone in our toxic journeys. I pray for faith though dear Lord. Allow us to faith it until we make it. In Jesus name I pray. Amen!

Whether you read this over the course of a month when you found time within your busy schedule, on an island to relax your mind or even during the course of one night when you couldn't go to sleep, I thank you. Sincerely, gracefully and respectfully. Thank you for listening to my thoughts because that is exactly what these were. It was me talking to you over a glass of wine, hoping that you heard and understood me. Thank you for allowing me to be vulnerable in my own way. I hope you now understand that you are not alone and that healing from your own toxic journey is easier than you thought it was in the beginning. I wish you well on your journey.

With Love,

Sam I Am.

Made in the USA
Columbia, SC
29 May 2025